Tahiti and its islands
Les Editions du Pacifique
10, avenue Bruat Papeete, Tahiti.

© Copyright by Société Nouvelle
des Editions du Pacifique, 1972, 1976, 1980, 1981, 1983.
Printed in Japan by Shumposha Photo Printing
Typeset in France by Publications-Elysées.
All rights reserved for all countries.

ISBN : 2-85700-171-1

tahiti
and its islands

text bob putigny

photography b. hermann · m. folco · c. rives · e. christian

*"In order to preserve the glamour of this dreamland,
I should have allowed it to remain untouched.
For those around me have spoiled my Tahiti,
trying to explain it according to their own ways.
They are those who drag along their empty characters,
their down-to-earth ideas, everywhere they go,
soiling all poetry with their mockery,
their own insensibility and their foolishness.
And civilisation has come here too often—
all our conventions, our habits, our vices.
And this wild poetry fades away,
with all the manners and traditions of the past."*

Pierre Loti

LES·EDITIONS·DU·PACIFIQUE

contents

There are two kinds of islands in Polynesia: high islands and low islands or atolls. The high islands are of basalt, volcanic in origin and the atolls are more or less circular rings of coral, often broken by channels and passes. According to Darwin's theory they were formed by an evolution in the reef structure which changed from "fringe" type to "barrier" type and then to an atoll.

As an example of high islands, we can see in the photo (above), Moorea, with Tahiti in the background.

Lost among the Leeward Islands, Tupai (opposite) is an atoll—one of the most beautiful in Polynesia.

french polynesia

Tahiti lies in the midst of the immense Pacific Ocean, which covers two thirds of the entire world. This name has become a magic word that designates not only the island itself, but also the group of islands that form French Polynesia. There are two kinds: the *high islands,* of volcanic origin, whose green peaks shoot up from the sea, and the *low islands* or *atolls,* thin rings of coral on which only a few coconut trees grow. They form five groups or archipelagos: Windward Islands, Leeward Islands, Tuamotu, Gambier, Marquesas and Austral. The meagre 4,000 km² that they cover are spread out over an area larger than that of Europe. Tahiti lies 9,000 km from Santiago and from Tokyo; 7,000 km from San Francisco; 4,000 km from Honolulu; 6,000 km from Sydney and 4,500 km from Auckland. Its position has made it a necessary stop-over in intercontinental or inter-island flights. Lying out of the cyclone zone, this paradise has only two seasons: one dry (from March to November), the other rainy (from November to March). The weather is always mild; the temperature varies between 70°F and 90°F. The water of the lagoon is warm: 73°F to 79°F.

The traveller today will not find here the mythical land where, in the words of the French explorer Bougainville "Venus is the goddess of hospitality". But he will discover a land of other riches, of a strange attraction which he will not be able to define. And like all others who have been here before him, he will try, but fail to understand the haunting charm of Tahiti.

underwater life

Polynesia possesses one of the most varied and spectacular under-water flora and fauna in the whole world. The diversity of species that live in these waters and the never-tiring beauty of the background are a constant surprise to the diver, the fisherman, the shell collector and the photographer. The lagoon hides, in its coral bushes and sandy floors, a bizarre multitude of living creatures: the quaint sea-urchins, the many-shaped and many-colored shells, the splendid lobsters, crabs and clams that are part of a native dinner. The largest number of species in the lagoon is that of the fish. The shark, lord of Polynesian waters, of a less agressive nature than its Australian cousins, shares its Kingdom with the sedentary bass and grouper that live in the calm waters. The soldierfish, the snapper and the armed surgeonfish, swim around in the colorful company of the parrotfish and wrasse, watched by the fierce muray eel, sentinel of these regions.

shells

After the fish, the principal attraction of this under-water world are the shells. The reefs and lagoons offer a large number of different surroundings that allow the various species to develop in the best possible conditions. They constitute a collector's dreamland, but the amateur must be aware of the danger of destroying the coral

From the most common species in the lagoon, the photographer has chosen (opposite from left to right) the colors of the chameleon sea bass, zebra surgeonfish, burnt parrotfish, blue-lined sea perch, royal angelfish. On the ocean side of the barrier reef, a black finned shark in search of prey, patrols tirelessly.

environment that the shells need for their growth and reproduction, and certain precautions must be taken so that life in these waters remains undisturbed. Industry has also a hand in the exploitation of shells: mother-of-pearl, usually collected for the nacre itself, is nowadays largely reserved for pearl culture. The troca shell, imported into Polynesia in 1957, is gathered by the ton during its short fishing season and is used in the making of souvenirs, buttons and small nacre objects. Shells have become the symbol of these islands, and it is a well-kept tradition that visitors leaving Tahiti receive shell necklaces as a farewell gift so that they will return some day to these enchanted shores.

In Polynesia, underwater fishing is not only a sport but a part of daily life. The Tahitians have perfected it: no useless massacre, but the family's meals are assured. One of the most pursued fish, here caught by Jean Tapu (opposite) world underwater-fishing champion, is the jack.
On the following double page, the main species of molluscs found in Polynesia have been photographed in their natural setting. From top to bottom and from left to right: a conch, a cone, a cowrie, a triton.

fauna and flora of the islands

The beauty and diversity of Polynesian flora vary according to each island. Atolls, having a calcareous and rather dry soil, possess a comparatively poor flora. Apart from the ever-present coconut tree, there is a low undergrowth —the *miki-miki*–, pandanus, sometimes breadfruit trees or *maiore* but rarely any flowers—*tiare* and periwinkle. On the contrary, on the high islands, such as Tahiti, the rich earth and the humidity are highly propitious to the growth of plants and trees. Except the mountains which are covered with scrub and fern trees, the exuberance of the vegetation is a wonderful surprise for the visitor who sees it for the first time. In the cool and damp valleys grow the *mape* or Tahitian chestnut-tree, bamboo, pandanus and *fei* or wild bananas; on the coast grow the coconut trees, breadfruit trees, mango trees, banana trees and above all, flowers. Apart from the native flowers of Tahiti *(tiare-tahiti* and *pua),* there are a multitude of other colorful flowers which enhance the gardens and hedges of the island: yellow creepers, flamboyants, red, pink and white hibiscus and the splendid bougainvillea. bougainvillea.

fauna

In Tahiti, as on the other islands of French Polynesia, there are none of the

Opposite from left to right and from top to bottom: copra decortication, the fruit of the breadfruit tree, a mango tree, a banana tree, a coconut tree, giant bamboos, a Tahitian chestnut tree. Following double page: Texas sage, hibiscus, bougainvillea, tiare tahiti, *frangipane, water lilies and orchids.*

extraordinary specimens of tropical fauna found throughout the world: no monkeys, no parrots, no giant snakes. Nor are there any dangerous or poisonous animals: only the centipede, whose sting is painful for some hours, and mosquitoes. Long ago, Polynesians brought pigs, poultry and dogs with them on their large outrigger canoes; rats and lizards came along as stowaways. Europeans imported a number of other domestic animals: horses, cows, cats, turkeys, etc. and also the Indian myna to destroy the wasps that fed on the fruit. The Indian myna preferred the fruit itself and its number has increased immensely—as well as that of the wasps. Birds from Asia, Africa, Australia and America have made their home on these islands and spread through the territory of French Polynesia. Nevertheless, seabirds—so useful to fishermen for finding shoals of fish—are becoming scarce in Tahiti, due to the growing human population on the coast. The most prolific, as well as the most interesting species, are found in the woodlands of the interior, and this forces Tahiti to seriously consider the problem of protection of its environment.
In all of French Polynesia there are some 90 birds species, of which 59 have been recorded in the Society Islands. The largest number are found in Tahiti, which because of its size and volcanic origin presents a variety of natural habitats. Since the arrival of the Europeans, several species have become extinct: *Cyanoramphus zealandicus,* a brightly coloured long—tailed parrot; *Rallus pacificus,* a red-billed rail, etc.

Opposite from left to right and from top to bottom: Tahiti kingfisher, crested or swift tern, reef heron, Tahiti flycatcher and a group of lesser golden plovers with a wandering tattler.

history

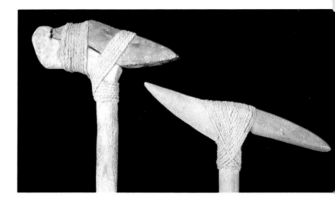

During the fifth century a.d., a group of adventurous Maori seamen crossed the ocean in outrigger canoes and discovered the island of Tahiti in its unspoiled splendor. It was not until June 1767 that the first Europeans arrived in Tahiti—Captain Wallis and his crew landed here, one year before the French Captain Bougainville. The Spaniard Mendana had already discovered the Marquesas in 1595 and the Portuguese Queiros the Tuamotu in 1606.

Captain Cook arrived in Tahiti on April 13, 1769, on board the *Endeavour,* and anchored in Matavai Bay. Together with the botanist Joseph Banks, he toured the island and after one week had acquired enough information to be able to draw an accurate map of Tahiti's coastline.

The artist Francis Parkinson wrote: "The land appeared as uneven as a piece of crumpled paper, being divided irregularly into hills and valleys; but a beautiful verdure covered both, even to the tops of the highest peaks". Cook understood that the name of the island was *Otaheite,* including the predicative "o" which means "it is". The Tahitians soon gave Cook and some of his crew Tahitianized surnames—Tute (Cook), Opane (Banks, the botanist), Tolano (Solander, a Swedish naturalist) and so on. Cook left Tahiti on July 13, 1769.

From top to bottom: two types of adze from Tahiti and the Austral Islands, a feminine ear-decoration and a bone tiki *both from the Marquesas Islands.*
On the right: the Arahurahu marae.

Above: the bust of Loti.
Opposite: a photo taken in 1870 of a Marquesan couple: already in contact with "civilisation" their eyes seem to see beyond things and beings.

the land of milk and honey

Tahitians knew nothing of writing or working in metal—or working at all, as the Europeans knew work. Their few needs were supplied by nature, aided perhaps by a few hours of physical strain every day or two. The rest of the time they spent in carefree bliss, in a state similar to the European conception of life in the garden of Eden.

Polynesian society was divided into several classes. The power of divine origin, was in the hands of the chiefs and priests, and was protected by a series of prohibitions or *tapu*. The violation of these *tapu* was severely punished. This system, based on the people's faith, served as a civil code and dispensed with a regular police force in a society that had no need for prisons.

As in every civilisation there were wars, in spite of the natural gentleness of the

Polynesian character—but these served the purpose of an immense game and also as a demographic regulator, adapted to the economic and social conditions of the islands.

The most mundane things reflected a natural poetic quality: in their dress, decorations and architecture. The Polynesian lifestyle, physical beauty of the people and the breathtaking scenery made Tahiti become everyman's dreamland in a very short time.

settlers in eden

People flocked in from all over the world: seamen and mutineers, smugglers and artists, puritans and quacks, businessmen and soldiers, adventurers and politicians. All took advantage of the islanders' hospitality, and many of their credulity. And after several conflicts between the European powers as to who would reign over these islands, France established its protectorate in 1842, during the reign of Pomare IV.

Nevertheless, it was not until 1880 that this protectorate was confirmed, under the reign of Pomare V, and today all the natives of French Polynesia are French citizens.

In order to improve agriculture on the island, 300 Chinese were brought to Tahiti. They soon abandoned the fields and became shopkeepers and most of the commerce is in their hands today. Nowadays more than 10,000 Asians live on the island, plus some 90,000 Tahitians and "demi-Tahitians" and 10,000 Europeans, called *popaa*.

Two congressmen, one senator and one economic and social counsellor represent this overseas territory in the French Government. The territory is administered by the High Commissioner, assisted by a five member council.

tahiti

Herman Melville, the famous author of *Moby Dick,* has left a perfect description of a traveller's discovery of Tahiti from aboard ship:
"Seen from the sea, the prospect is magnificent. It is one mass of shaded tints of green, from beach to mountain-top; endlessly diversified with valleys, ridges, glens and cascades. The loftiest peaks cast their shadows over the ridges and down into the valleys. At the head of these, waterfalls glitter in the sunlight as if pouring through vertical bowers of verdure. Such an enchanted air breathes over the whole that it seems a fairyland, fresh and pure from the hand of the Creator. The picture becomes no less attractive upon nearer approach. It is no exaggeration to say that a European of any sensibility who wanders into the valleys for the first time, away from the haunts of the natives, sees every object as if in a dream, owing to the ineffable repose and beauty of the landscape; for a while, he almost refuses to believe that scenes like these should have a commonplace existence."
But unfortunately Tahiti is no longer discovered from the sea. In most cases visitors arrive by plane—one of the many international aircrafts that land daily at Faaa airport.
Nevertheless, the view from the air is equally breath-taking. First Moorea, then Tahiti in the background and finally the emerald-green lagoon at the foot of the giant crags: a unique and unforgettable spectacle.

Tahiti is becoming more and more tourist-minded.
Tahiti-Faaa Airport now receives most large
planes and "charters" which make it possible
for many to visit the islands. With these flights
Tahiti has ceased to be an isolated island.
In spite of the growing number of tourists debark-
ing at Tahiti, very few stay here. The majority
go to the inhabited islands which are considered
to be slightly less "civilised".
There are two airlines wich have regular services
between the islands: Air Polynesia and Air Tahiti
(photo above). the latter flies to Moorea many times a
day and also to the Leewards Islands, the Marquesas
the Austral Islands.

papeete

The capital of French Polynesia
(40,000 inhabitants) is built on the
north-western coast of Tahiti, at the foot
of a green mountain-range. Everything
is centered in Papeete: the High
Commissioner's residence, the territorial
assembly, banks, tourist office,
travel agencies, post office, supermarkets
and Chinese shops, hotels, cinemas,
night clubs, two hospitals and a large
number of restaurants, both European
and Chinese.

Since the building of the international
airport and the settling of the Pacific
Experimentation Center, the aspect of
the city has changed—some say for the
worse. The little police headquarters
with servicemen in colonial uniforms,
on a shady street of provincial charm, has
been replaced by a large cement building
in a fairly modern city of noisy traffic,
sprouting traffic lights and
over-crowded parking lots. Trees have
been replaced by lamp-posts, grass and
flowers by asphalt streets and the stars
by neon signs.

Tahitians have become accustomed to
tourism; money has created a proletariat.
Simple pleasures and easy life have been
transformed to adapt to the false needs
of a consumer society and the artificial
urges of politics, paid labor and
luxuries. Progress has had its way.
Nevertheless, there is still a faint glimmer
of that innocent bliss. Along the quay,
yachts from all over the world tell of the
dream that people still hope to find in
Tahiti. And Papeete, even though
transformed, is the first step into one of
man's truest havens.

*Papeete: the cathedral, the Governor's residence,
the sea-front, the Assembly, the tourist bureau
and a bird's-eye view of the city.*

map of papeete

The reputation which the Tahi
tians have for laziness is, if yo
visit Papeete, often contradic
ed by the activity seen by da
and by night in the streets ar
on the quays of the town.
Nowadays the traditional occu
pations have been joined b
those of a modern expandir
town. On the seafront, wome
can be seen making crown
and garlands of flowers whic
they display either on th
ground or on the painted woo
en stalls used for curios: shel
mother-of-pearl, trunk-fis.
sculpted and varnished coc
nuts, hats, plaited pandan
mats, carved, wooden bow
and tiki: all the local crafts.
On the ferry quay, you can wa
peacefully, sitting on the sac
of copra for the departure whic
is always delayed. Near th
market, you squeeze yourse
onto one of the "trucks", th
local buses which will stop f
you anywhere along the road.

the market

The marketplace is not only the "stomach" of Papeete: it is also its heart. Everything is kept spotlessly clean: no bad smells amongst the gleaming fish, the pyramids of papaya, the striped watermelons, the green and yellow mangoes.

Here is the meeting-place of Polynesians from all over the islands and the true center of Polynesian life in the city. The arrival of the fish is the highlight of the market activities, twice a day: at 5 a.m. and at 4 p.m.

The quantities of fruit and vegetables may surprise the visitors: it usually represents the entire harvest of a month and comes straight from the neighboring islands. The farmer who arrives in Papeete to sell his crop, sleeps either at his parents' house (if they live in Papeete) or in the large hall beside the market, which is transformed during the night into an immense bedroom in which everyone spreads out his own mat and sleeps till dawn. Then they wash and in the midst of much hustle and bustle all these voluntary exiles cross over the road and have a cup of black coffee and *firi-firi* or local doughnuts in one of the many cafés around the market. Towards 4 or 5 a.m. the "trucks" or local buses arrive, bringing the farmers and grocers from the districts into Papeete. Sometimes these "trucks" leave the night before, sometimes stopping along the peninsular road to pick up a fisherman who is late, or some hurried housewife locking up her pigs and chickens.

There is no bargaining in the market: prices are previously established and are not to be discussed.

On the roads alongside the market the "trucks" line up waiting to be loaded with goods and passengers.

The two main products sold in Papeer
market are fish and watermelon. Peop
from all the surrounding islands meet at th
market place to sell one of the best-loved loc
products: watermelons.

Today, Tahiti alone cannot supply all the fis
required for the daily needs and so much
imported from the other islands, especial
from the Tuamotu Archipelago...

The market has become one of the la
tourist attractions in the center of the tow
and represents, for the Polynesians, a livin
witness of the kind of commerce to whic
they are attached, because of its huma
characteristics and the style of life that
creates throughout the islands.

Fish, which comes from the open sea or the lagoon, is eaten in many ways: steamed, barbecued, but the most usual is raw. To prepare raw fish (photo opposite), you need a bonito, tuna or a parrot-fish: remove the skin, cut the flesh into fillets and then into cubes. Pour lime juice over the fish, salt and leave it to marinate for about ten minutes, drain off most of the juice and add some vegetables, e.g. chopped carrots, tomatoes; pour on coconut milk and serve chilled. Another recipe for raw fish, fafaru (photo above) is to put a fish into a bowl, cover it with sea water and let it macerate for 2 to 3 days. Then strain the juice and pour it over some fresh fish that has been washed, cleaned and cut into pieces. Leave this to macerate for at least 6 hours, to taste!

circle island tour

Tahitians are not too keen on mechanics but adore cars. There are an incredible number of cars in Tahiti, in spite of there being only one road around the island. Most of them are large sports models—perfectly useless on an island where speed is limited to 50 miles an hour. In spite of this, Tahitians usually race down straight bits of road and accidents are not infrequent. But it is mainly a form of local snobbery: the length of a car is directly related to the importance of its owner and disproportionate to the size of the island.

Some of these large noisy metal beasts are only brought out on Sundays: the day of the circle island tour. Head to tail, sports cars, mini-buses, "trucks", motorbikes, bicycles and scooters race around the island from morning till evening.

Tourists are therefore advised to select another day for this traditional excursion. The entire tour (120 km) usually starts from Papeete and runs clockwise round the island.

The tour given here does not include Tahiti Iti or Small Tahiti—the peninsula. It is possible to drive only 18 km along either coast of this part of Tahiti, but there is a road from Taravao village which leads up onto a plateau from which there is a splendid view of Tahiti Nui—Big Tahiti.

The most beautiful sand beach in Tahiti is at Punaauia (opposite) between the 15th and 18th kilometers of the circle island tour.

Following page: the mountainside is being cut into by bulldozers and disfigured by housing estates, causing landslides in certain areas owing to deforestation, polluting the lagoon and killing the coral with mud.

At 4 km is *Arue,* were the last king of Tahiti, Pomare V and his ancestors and family are buried. Next is the *Tahara'a* Hill and built on its side, facing the sea, is the hotel that bears the same name: there is a beautiful view of Moorea in the distance, and Matavai Bay with Point Venus cutting into the sea. *Point Venus* (turning left at km 10) got its name because Captain Cook came here in 1769 to observe the passing of this planet across the sun. On the site where the first explorers landed in Tahiti a museum has been built showing wax figures of several historical characters.

Km 22 brings us to the *Tiarei Blow-hole,* a natural formation in the rocks through which the waves crash, letting out a jet of water that sometimes splashes on to the road. Some 100 meters farther on is the *Faarumai valley* where three high cascades fall into a true tropical wilderness below. *Hitiaa,* at km 39, has a bronze sign indicating the site where Bougainville arrived in 1768. After the *Faatautia waterfall*—which can be seen from the road (km 42)—we arrive at the *peninsula of Taiarapu* (km 55). The tip of this beautiful area, which gives an idea of what Tahiti must have been like in the golden era, can only be visited by foot or from the sea, by boat (see photo page 44—45). To return to Papeete from Taravao, the road leads on to the west coast, less wild than the east coast. After *Phaeton port,* we arrive at *Papeari,* the flower district (km 49,5) where the beautiful *botanical gardens* lie in all their splendor. They were created in 1937 by Harrison Smith. 9 km further on is the golf course of *Atimaono.*

There are two ancient Tahitian temples. or *marae* to be visited: that of *Mahaiatea* (km 39) on the coast, the largest in all Polynesia, unfortunately in ruins; and

after the *Maraa cave* (km 28,5) the *Marae Arahurahu* in *Paea* (km 22,5) that has been cleverly re-built by the Society of Oceanic Studies.

Next come the residential area of *Punaauia*, the *Maeva Beach* and *Beachcomber Hotels* (Km 8) and after passing *Faaa international airport* we return to our point of departure: *Papeete*.

Some scenes from the island tour: the "truck" being washed in the river, Point Venus lighthouse, a tiki at the Gauguin Museum, the Museum of the Discovery created to commemorate the first navigators who landed at Tahiti: the Maoris in the fifth Century, then Wallis, Bougainville and Cook at the end of the eighteenth century.

47

In olden days, the Tahitians lived mostly in the deep valleys in the interior of the island. The Tahiti of today, with houses climbing further and further up the sides of the mountains, is very different from what the first navigators saw. Coffee and vanilla, which were cultivated intensively here, have now almost disappeared but,

from June to August, the traditional harvest of wild oranges deep in the Punaruu and Mahina valleys still takes place as in ancient times.
It is better to discover Tahiti's valleys, plateaus and risers on foot.
Opposite: the "Blow Hole" and Lake Vahiria.

Below: east coast shoreline.

Tahiti, without becoming another Hawaii, is being modernised. Concrete has largely replaced local building materials: bamboo and plaited coconut palms. Coming back into fashion are the houses inherited from the colonial era, of painted wood with large verandas and roofs of corrugated iron. Below, left: a Papeete street at the end of the last century.

art in tahiti

The name of Gauguin is linked to that of
Tahiti for ever. The ten years he spent
here and in the Marquesas gave to his
work a precise and unmistakeable style.
The Gauguin Museum, a memorial to
his genius, was created and is still
supported by the Singer-Polignac
Foundation. It shows reproductions of
his paintings and of the objects that
surrounded him, tracing his life through
a number of contemporary photographs.
The Museum is also open for exhibitions
by local artists, conferences and concerts.
The visitor to Tahiti is often shocked to
find that there is only one original
painting Gauguin left on the island. The
fact is that during his lifetime, no one in
Tahiti bought Gauguin's paintings.
Gauguin himself must have received the
same kind of shock when he arrived in
1891 looking for true ancient Polynesian
art. Having been quickly converted to
Christianity, the Tahitians had destroyed
most of their temples, sculptures and
even everyday objects, and Gauguin
found hardly any vestiges of their art.
Nowadays some *tiki,* petroglyphs and
sundry objects can be seen at the
Papeete Museum, and a few *marae* have
been restored. The Tourist Board has
undertaken the reconstruction of several
marae on Moorea and in the Leeward
Islands, so the tourist can have an idea
of what this civilisation was like in the
days before the discovery. Local crafts
have again come to life, and the visitor
can purchase wooden sculptures,
shellcraft and a local kind of patchwork
called *tifaifai.*

*Until recently only copies and reproductions
were exhibited at the Gauguin Museum (opposite).*

tahitians

"The very air the people breathe, their songs, their dances... all conspire to call to mind the sweets of love, and all engage to give themselves up to them. Thus accustomed to live continually immersed in pleasure, the people of Tahiti have acquired a witty and humorous temper, which is the offspring of ease and joy." **L.-A. Bougainville**

Bougainville wrote that he had never seen a race of men of such perfect proportions, "ideal models for Hercules and Mars". Philibert de Commerson compared the women to Greek goddesses and called them "sisters of the Graces". Tahitians, however, are not just copies of classical beauty, but have a comeliness of their own. Broad shoulders, flat and strong back, round hips, big feet (which give them a superb balance), delicate skin, thick black hair, full pleasing lips and large eyes. They pass easily from sorrow to joy and they seem to be constantly surprised by everything. They look upon the spectacle of modern life with resignation and slight bewilderment. They are not aggressive nor spiteful against the *popaa,* the foreigners; they rather consider them with slight irony and lack of understanding of *popaa* ways, as if they felt that they belonged to a simpler, happier world that has been hidden from them and that comes back at times in a song, a dance, a perfumed drink. Tahitians understand life to be essentially a pursuit of happiness. Work is not a goal, it is simply the means to get certain commodities. Time is the true wealth. Bougainville had already noticed this, when leaving Tahiti he wrote with melancholy: "Farewell happy and wise people... Stay always as you are now..."

Portraits of Tahitians: mamaruau *and young girls after mass; men from Bora Bora in their Sunday best.*

sports

The population of Tahiti is mostly young and vigorous, and all kinds of sports have become very popular amongst them. Several stadiums have been built to satisfy the increasing demand.

Football is one of the most popular. It used to be played barefooted, but lately it has improved and the aim is to obtain an international level. Next in importance is boxing, which allows a full expression of the Tahitian's strength and nimbleness, and attracts an enthusiastic public.

The long waves of Papara and Papenoo offer splendid oportunities for surfing. This is the traditional Tahitian sport. Even in the times of Sir Joseph Banks,

Surfing is probably the most popular sport in Tahiti, but on the other islands football, volley-ball and basket-ball are just as popular. Opposite: a lively game in the Marquesas.

the British naturalist who accompanied Cook on his voyage around the world, surfing was a widely-spread sport in Polynesia. Banks called it "their favorite game".

All other water-sports are equally popular: swimming, diving, canoe racing and sailing on the lagoon.

the *vahine*

"The girl was fully as fair and had as good features as the generality of women in England, and had she been dressed after the English manner, I am certain no man would have thought her of another country."

George Robertson, 1767

The *vahine,* romantic symbol of a mythical Tahiti, has changed a little over the years. Bougainville, a connoisseur of beautiful women, wrote that "their faces are as beautiful as that of any European woman and their bodies much more so. The Tahitian Venus is goddess of hospitality and her cult has no mysteries on this island. Alas, our customs have forbidden our true enjoyment of all this!" The beautiful girls that used to swim around the ships to greet the sailors with their flowers and their smiles, can no longer fulfil their mermaid's task. Too many tourists flock into Tahiti today and the legendary *vahine* has become one with the sirens and the fairies. Nowadays they work in banks or import-export offices, but their marvellous faces and figures are still a thing of beauty in the busy streets, as they were on Gauguin's sunny beaches.

belief

Polynesians possessed an important and precise mythology that speaks of their imagination and poetical genius.

The traditional picture of a vahine tahiti: *pareu, a flower behind her ear and her languorous indolence.*

Traditional knowledge was in the hands of the priests who had great authority in Tahitian society. They believed in the immortality of the soul and that after their death they would be taken to a heavenly paradise, *te havaiki* or else become another creature "on land, in the sea or in the skies". They worshipped one god, creator of the whole universe, source of all knowledge and power. His name was Taaroa and he was assisted by secondary gods born from himself, and other divinities.

The religious ceremonies took place in square rooms of sculpted stone or coral slab walls, depending on the island. At one end was the altar and it was there that the idols were sanctified and the rare human sacrifices took place. Nothing is left today of this social and religious organization and the surviving elements of Polynesian culture can only be seen in museums and private collections.

The profound religious sense of the Polynesian people has turned nowadays towards the Christian religions: Protestant in Tahiti and the Leeward Islands and Catholic in the Tuamotu and the Marquesas. The only Tahitian book is the Bible, translated by King Pomare II. They have a great respect for the teachings of Christian dogma and obey all ten commandments—with the sole exception, perhaps, of the sixth, as they cannot bring themselves to consider physical love as a source of sin. They are naturally generous, never greedy, hardly jealous and they never swear. They attend mass regularly and enjoy dressing up for the occasion. Their singing in church is mostly based on ancient Polynesian melodies with words added by the missionaries.

Paofai Temple in Papeete (opposite) and a wedding at Bora Bora (following page).

the feast

"**Tonight we will put scarlet flowers in our hair and sing strange, slumbrous South Sea songs to the concertina, and drink red French wine, and dance and bathe in a soft lagoon by moonlight, and eat great squelchy tropical fruits.**"

Rupert Brooke

Tahitians call it "bringue" (pronounced "brrrangg"... from the French argot) and the word designates a sort of folkloric celebration in which everyone drinks, sings and makes merry. Guitars, crowns of flowers and bottles of beer are the typical ingredients of this feast for any occasion.

The "bringue" takes place at any time: Saturday evening after visiting the many night-clubs and discos, Sunday morning on the island tour, a wedding or a birthday, an official holiday or an informal friendly gathering.

songs

"Crown the hair, and come away!
Hear the calling of the moon,
And the whispering scents that stray
About the idle warm lagoon."
                    Rupert Brooke

Singing is present in all Tahitian activities
and it accompanies their whole day, from
morning to night.

All occasions are an excuse for singing:
religious ceremonies, feasts, burials,
"bringues", a walk down the road or
a picnic on the beach.

Whenever a group of Tahitians gets
together, a song rises from it like a
harmonious, traditional voice. Tahitians
carry singing in their blood.

Any tune can be sung: folkloric songs,
the latest American or European hits,
songs by some new Tahitian talent—
all in Tahitian words which seem to
fit any kind of music.

Sometimes they form large choral
groups or *himene.* Many of the vocal
selections are ancient Polynesian tunes,
handed down through the ages, as
writing was unknown to them. There
are the *tarava* that tell historical or
legendary tales; the *fango* or death songs
of the Tuamotu, and many others.

The singing of the *fango,* for instance,
is accompanied by the sounding of a horn
made with the hands held in a certain
position over the mouth, producing a
gruff monotonous note, while the men
sway backwards and forwards. The
women sing the litany in which each
part ends with a low long sound, like
the last breath of life. In the *ute* men and
women form a small group that sings
certain rhymes in a guttural voice. A
soloist interrupts with comical or

*All you need for a party in Tahiti is a guitar, a
ukulele and some beer!*
*Following double page: javelin thrower at the
July celebrations.*

satirical remarks.
Finally certain songs are sung by the choir during the dances, and tell tales of love, war and adventure: *aparima, hivinau, paoa*.

the july celebrations

The noisy crowd that on a fine July day in 1789 ran out into the streets of Paris and stormed the mighty Bastille, starting off the events that are known today as the French Revolution, would have been very surprised to learn that two centuries later the Tahitians (who had only just come into appearance in the European world of the eighteenth century) commemorate their deeds for three consecutive weeks of "bringue" on a national scale: country balls, shooting and lottery booths, merry-go-rounds, drinking bouts, canoe races, javelin throwing contests, coconut husking contests and above all, dancing and singing competitions between selected groups from all the islands.

dances

Dancing is the Tahitian's most natural and most spontaneous form of expression. They are never tired, never bored of dancing, never *fiu* or fed up. If on a Papeete street or in some remote corner of one of the districts, the frantic rhythm of the wooden drums *(toere)* suddenly springs to life, everyone—men, women, children—leave whatever they are doing and rush out to watch, with a critical eye, the well-beloved dances of Tahiti.
There are several kinds of dances. The *otea,* a quick warrior dance; *aparima,* a languid and lascivious dance; *hivinau,* danced in a ring; *paoa,* satirical dance in which the dancers clap their hands to the tune; *ori-tahiti* or *tamure,* in which

men shake their knees violently and women mimic the gestures of love. The botanist Joseph Banks noted in his *Endeavour* Journal in August 1769, "Musick is very little known to them which is the more wonderfull as they are very fond of it. They have only two instruments the flute and the drum. ... They dance especially the young girls whenever they can collect 8 or 10 together, singing most indecent words using most indecent actions and setting their mouths askew in a most extraordinary manner, in the practise of which they are brought up from their earlyest childhood; in doing this they keep time to a surprizing nicety, I might almost say as true as any dancers I have seen in Europe tho their time is certainly much more simple. This exercise is however left off as soon as they arrive at Years of maturity for as soon as ever they have formed a connection with a man they are expected to leave of Dancing *Timorodee* as it is called."

A group of himene *from Mataiea (opposite). Following double page: a dance spectacle at a hotel in Moorea.*

moorea

Linked forever with Tahiti's landscape, rising like a shark's jaw from the sea, Moorea lies 20 km to the west of its neighboring island. Moorea is less "civilized": less traffic, no parking lots, no electricity, no parking meters. Instead it has preserved the grace of its colonial buildings, beautiful houses with pandanus or palmtree roofs. Coffee and vanilla are no longer the island's principal resources. They have been replaced by the *tiare tahiti,* the small perfumed flower that has become the symbol of Tahiti. Tourism has reached the island and several fine hotels have been built. The Club Méditerranée, a village set up on a splendid white sand beach, is one of the most accomplished of its kind. The organisers have taken

Moorea, opposite, 5,000 inhabitants, sister island and a week-end escape for the people in Tahiti, with a regular boat and plane service.
Above: a very common bird in Polynesia, the red-footed booby.

special care to protect the environment, incorporating the traditional hut-building style with the comforts required by the modern traveller. 550 visitors can stay at the Club Méditerranée, and take advantage of the numerous sports that are offered to them: tennis, water skiing, deep-sea diving, canoe excursions and visits round the island in a glass-bottom boat. There are also several shows of Tahitian dancing and singing.

Flying to Moorea from Tahiti takes only 7 minutes and there are flights leaving every 10 or 20 minutes from Faaa. But discovering Moorea from the sea through the pass of Pao Pao Bay is one of the most extraordinary spectacles that this world has to offer, and should not be missed on any account.

Two bays cut into the north coast of Moorea: Pao Pao (or Cook's Bay) and Opunohu. These two natural formations, with their sharp coastlines and splendid colors, curiously shaped rocks and exuberant vegetation, provide a unique sight for the visitors.

However, now even Moorea is changing. The vanilla which at one time covered the hillsides has completely disappeared. Many workers commute between Moorea and Tahiti, and the island comes alive at the week-end. They sing, dance and most important of all, they relax. There is a road 60 km long leading to the beautiful sites all around the island, that preserves an old-fashioned charm now lost in Tahiti. Many lovers of that charm have left the bigger island and have now settled on Moorea.

Scenes from daily life on Moorea: the beach at the Club Méditerranée, Afareaitu church, a child holding a mango, an aerial view of the two bays, a group of children, and following double page, Opunohu Bay.

the leeward islands

The Leeward Archipelago is so named because it lies some 200 kilometers to the north-west of Tahiti, i.e. away from the dominant winds (the trade-winds from east north-east). It was discovered by Captain Cook, after his first voyage, in 1769. There are five high islands: Raiatea, Tahaa, Huahine, Bora Bora and Maupiti and four atolls : Tupai, Mopelia, Scilly and Bellinghausen.

raiatea

Because of its size (280 km²) and because of its history (the Maori migrations settled here before spreading throughout the Pacific), Raiatea is the most important of the Leeward Islands. The principal town, Uturoa (2,800 inhabitants) is the administrative capital of the archipelago, with post-office, bank, hotels, hospital and cinema, plus a lively market and several Chinese shops. Mount Tapioi rises behind the town and port up to 300 m and from its peak one can see an extraordinary panorama of islands, mountains and lagoons. 30 km to the south lies the small village of Opoa, principal site of ancient Polynesian culture, with the ruins of the gigantic *marae* Taputapuatea, where the Maori gods had their thrones. Thanks to the lack of beaches all along its coast, Raiatea has escaped the tourist invasion. Only certain *motu* or islets serve as camping sites for nudists or improvised banquets. And during the July celebrations, Uturoa offers a less sophisticated spectacle than that of Papeete: during the three week festival laughter, singing and dancing accompany the sound of wooden drums and tightly strung guitars.

On the side of the sacred mountain Temehani where, it is said, the spirits of the departed live, the "Tiare Apetahi" grows in abundance. The buds of this plant open at sunrise with what sounds like small explosions. Many efforts have been made to cultivate this plant elsewhere, but up to now they have failed completely.

Opposite: the motu *at the Teavapiti pass opposite Uturoa and Hurepiti Bay at Tahaa.*
Above: the overloaded boats are the only means of communication between Tahaa and Raiatea.

tahaa

Tahaa and Raiatea are sister islands: that is, they share the same lagoon, surrounded by several green islets. There is no road on Tahaa, which adds to its natural charm. In the small cemetery of Vaitoare village Rarahu is buried, the child-bride of *Le mariage de Loti,* the bestselling XIX century novel by French author Pierre LOTI. Another village, Patio, is well known for the skill of its canoes' crews.

huahine

Huahine is in fact two islands: Huahine-Nui in the north and Huahine-Iti in the south. Both lie in the same lagoon, surrounded by the same barrier reef. They are united by a bridge across a shallow channel that can be crossed on foot during low tide. Two extinct volcanoes, Turi and Puhuerei, rise over the islands like protecting gods. The coastline is very uneven, with white sand beaches scattered all along, from which the beautiful lagoon can be enjoyed in the uttermost calm. The principal town, Fare, is a picturesque group of Polynesian houses at the foot of Mount Turi. The greatest attraction of this island is probably Maeva Lake. A village on stilts has been built in its waters and the many-colored bamboo huts reflected on the peaceful lake are a splendid sight. Nearby, at the foot of Mount Tapu or "sacred mountain", several *marae* ruins tell of the glorious past. The many aspects of this double-island make it a true rival of another Polynesian beauty: Bora Bora.

bora bora

Bora Bora is the best known and most praised of the Leeward Islands. It is the island that the famous navigator Alain Gerbault chose as his final port and eternal resting place, and it has always been a favorite haven for writers and movie-makers interested in the South Pacific. Rising out of the green lagoon, Mount Paia (661 m) looms over the village of Vaitape, the administrative center of the island. Along the 35 km road that circles the island there are several places of interest: Point Matira, for instance, next to the Bora Bora Hotel, with a fine white sand beach; also the two other villages—Anau and Faanui. Amongst the 2,000 inhabitants of Bora Bora are some of the best fishermen and dancers of the whole South Seas.

An aerial view of Bora Bora with the famous triangular-shaped Motu Tapu, in the foreground. Following page: Matira Point, one of the most beautiful beaches in Polynesia.

maupiti

Maupiti is certainly one of the wonders
of the ocean. It is a small closed universe
that has been able to preserve all the
beauty and peace of times gone by. Its
200 m high peaks are constantly
surrounded by white sea birds and at the
mountain foot a thick vegetation of
tropical trees and dazzling flowers try to
hide the fishermen's huts, the *marae*
ruins and the little village of Vaiea. The
glittering lagoon is protected from the
ocean waves by a thin strip of sand where
coconut trees grow and where the
600 inhabitants of the island keep a
plantation of watermelons.

the tuamotu islands

According to Tahitian mythology, the Maori god Tukerai (a sort of Hercules and Neptune, all in one), tried one day to shake the sea. The result was a terrible storm and out of the deep waters rose a series of islands, spread out along 1,500 km: the Tuamotu archipelago. Magellan crossed the area without seeing a single one: a true miracle. They were discovered in 1605 by the Portuguese Queiros and were called "the dangerous archipelago" by Bougainville.

the dangerous archipelago

Thousands of ships have sunk after crashing into the reef that suddenly rises out of nowhere to meet them; thousands have had their planks ripped off by the sharp coral teeth.
Every other year or so one of the inter-island ferries "rides the reef", as the natives call it, and sinks into the ocean. Nowadays there are charts, nautical handbooks and precise instruments to help the navigators through the passes, but in the past they had to depend upon their compasses and instinct. From 1770 to 1809, 12 large ships—European and American—ran into the murderous reef. Archeological researches made on Amanu atoll have discovered the remains of the San Lesmés, an early XVI century caravel that also became a victim of the hidden coral.

Previous pages: the unloading of the ferry is the most typical and representative spectacle of the isolation in which this archipelago lives.
Opposite: the Tahiti lorikeet, although on the way to extinction, is present on many atolls in the Tuamotu Archipelago. On the contrary, the great frigatebird (above) is common throughout Polynesia.

the atolls

Of the 77 islands that form the Tuamotu archipelago, all but one are atolls. These thin round strips of sand and coral, crowned with slim coconut trees, encircle emerald lagoons in which fish, shellfish, shells and mother-of-pearl live in perfect harmony. The poor soil is scarcely apt for agriculture, and the inhabitants live on copra and fishing.

There is no fresh water, except for an occasional brackish pool and rain water that is caught and stored in stone basins. Some of the atolls have no way out to the sea; others have one or several passes through which the ships can come and take refuge in the lagoon.

The entire archipelago has a population of 6,000. Many atolls are not inhabited, except in the fishing and copra collecting seasons.

The atolls are a haven of peace and quiet. No sound is heard except the thunder of the breaking waves, the fall of a coconut on the sand and the shrill cry of the sea-birds. No sight is seen except water and light that seem to arise from the dawn of Creation.

The only high island of the archipelago is Makatea, a mineral block with a surface of 28 km², only some sixty meters thick, a floating mass in the deep blue ocean. Its white cliffs and its pierced rocks hide a layer of phosphate that has not been exploited since 1966. A curious sight is the 7 km long railway line, with its engine rusting in the rain and sun, abandoned to the birds and the eerie lunar landscape.

On the atolls, the imagination as much as the eye is struck by the intensity of the blues of the sea and sky, which blend together along an indefinite line from which emerge the soft green of the coconut trees and the agressive whitness of the coral sand beaches.

pearl culture

But the other islands of the Tuamotu archipelago are coming to life again. The mother-of-pearl industry had declined since 1950, due to the invention of polyester and the extinction of the pearl oyster banks. But in the last few years a new demand for mother-of-pearl has arisen all over the world, for the production of buttons and souvenirs. Another successful enterprise is the grey pearl culture, the *poe rava,* of a dark grey or greenish color unique in the world. It seems that long ago the beds of many lagoons were covered with valuable pearl oysters. The men could wade into the waist-deep water of the lagoons and pick up hundreds of kilogrammes a day. As these shallow beds became depleted the men began to dive, going deeper and deeper. As late as 1910 the only aid the local divers needed was a lead weight or heavy stone tied to a rope. In this way the divers, who did not wear masks, could descend more rapidly. Naturally the supplies did not last long. Realizing what would happen, the French aid program — FIDES — started, in 1968, to organize and finance a scheme aimed at developing new but simple methods of cultivating the pearl oysters and urging the local islanders to use them on a commercial scale. There are pearl farms on Manihi, Takapoto and Marutea-South atolls.

Scenes from daily life in the Tuamotu Archipelago, above: the small rusty train at Makatea.
The main street in Tiputa village on the atoll of Rangiroa.
An old Ford which would be a collector's delight, still carries sacks of copra up and down the road — a few hundred meters long.
Following double page: a whale-boat carrying copra.

the gambier archipelago

The Tuamotu archipelago is followed to the south-east by a round and vast lagoon containing several islands that form the Gambier archipelago. Amongst these are four large high islands. The soil there is not very fertile but the waters off the coast are rich in all kinds of fish.

The principal island is Mangareva, some 30 km round. Its highest peak, Mount D'Uff, reaches 400 m. The principal village is Rikitea, capital of the archipelago.

Mangareva is the only inhabited island. The other three, Aakararu, Aukena and Taravai, once inhabited, are now deserted. All of them have large stone churches built in a European style, a reminder of the past century in which Father Laval brought the gospel to these islands and became a sort of absolute ruler till his death in 1880.

The few inhabitants that are left (560, compared to the 7,000 in the times of the missionaries), the ruins that spring from the wilderness, the strange wild landscape, awake in the traveller a feeling of nostalgic melancholy.

Local legends of Mangareva claim a connection between that island and Easter Island — some 1,500 miles east of the Gambiers. The natives took a rock and sculpted it into a ship, called "Poatuto", in which 600 warriors were flown to Easter Island, conquered the island and returned.

The Gambier Archipelago lives out of time, in the nostalgia created by an amazing past to which the ruins (opposite) and the grandeur of a cathedral with its solemn processions, bear witness.

the marquesas

1,500 km north of Tahiti lie the Marquesas, a group of some ten steep green islands without a lagoon. They are divided into two groups: the northern group, including the largest island, Nukuhiva and its capital, Taiohae; and the southern group, including Hivaoa and its capital Atuona, where Gauguin—who died in 1903—was buried. Being nearer to the Equator, the climate of the Marquesas is hotter and more humid than that of Tahiti. The population is approximately 6,000.

The Marquesas Islands are distinguished by their often desolate countryside. Opposite: Hane Bay. The horse has remained the only means of transport (following double page). Gauguin is buried at Atuona (above) where he spent the last years of his life.

the austral archipelago

The Austral archipelago lies the farthest south of all the islands in French Polynesia. It is formed by five high islands: Tubuai, the largest, discovered by Cook in 1777, has a 23 km road that runs around the island. The capital is Mataura. The houses are made of coral bricks and tin roofs, and the inhabitants travel on horseback. One can still see the fortified site where the *Bounty* mutineers anchored their ship before sailing off to Pitcairn Island. Rurutu island has no coastal road: only high mountain paths that can be followed on horseback, across crags 400 m above sea level. Avera village is a typical site, with its taro plantations and its square white houses. Eric de Bischop lived here and according to his last wishes, was buried in Moerai cemetery ("Moerai" means "heaven of dreams"). Rimatara, a small island, has its own history: together with Rurutu it formed an independant kingdom that only became part of French Polynesia in 1935. There are no natural harbors on the island, but a few very fine white sand beaches. The most beautiful of the Austral archipelago is probably Raivavae, with its luminous lagoon. Unfortunately, there is no road around it to visit the entire island. The prettiest girls in Polynesia are said to come from Raivavae. The ancient inhabitants used to be very tall and well built and a few stone *tiki* tell of this forgotten past. Finally Rapa, the island farthest south

The arrival of the ferry at Rapa and (following page) on Sundays—they show off their many colored dresses and marvellous hats just as proudly as in Papeete.

(27°) lies 1,000 km from Tahiti. The weather here is almost cold and the general aspect of the island is rather grey and melancholic. Rapa stands at the very frontier of the "roaring forties", the strong southern winds. Several Maori fortifications guard the central bay from a height of 700 m. There is only one village, Haueri, and more women than men on the island. No coconut trees grow here because of the climate, but taro and other vegetables adapt easily to the fertile soil.

All sorts of imported fruits and vegetables are grown in Rapa: asparagus, cabbages, potatoes, coffee and raspberries. But due to the infrequent communications with Papeete (one boat a month) exportation is a difficult, almost impossible task.

useful information

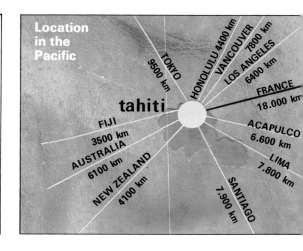

Location in the Pacific

tahiti

TOKYO 9500 km
HONOLULU 4400 km
VANCOUVER 7800 km
LOS ANGELES 6400 km
FRANCE 18.000 km
ACAPULCO 6.600 km
LIMA 7.800 km
SANTIAGO 7.900 km
NEW ZEALAND 4100 km
AUSTRALIA 6100 km
FIJI 3500 km

French Polynesia

French Polynesia consists of 4,000 km² of islands scattered over 4 million km² of ocean.
There are 117 islands divided into 5 archipelagos: the Society Islands, which consist of the Windward Islands (Tahiti, Moorea...) and of the Leeward Islands Huahine, Raiatea, Bora Bora...); the Marquesas Islands; the Austral Islands; the Tuamotu Islands; the Gambier Islands. These islands are either high and volcanic or low and of coral origin.

local time
Local time is GMT-10. French Polynesia is 2 hours behind San Francisco, 5 hours behind New York and 11 hours behind Paris.

climate
Tropical, hot and humid, cooled by the trade winds. There are two seasons: one mainly dry and cool, from March to November (70°F to 80°F); the other hot and humid, from November to March (80°F to 95°F).

flora
Sub-tropical. Specially exuberant along the coast and in the valleys: coconut, mango, breadfruit, flamboyant, bougainvillea, frangipani, *tiare* and many others. On the mountainside the vegetation is poorer and more indigenous: casuarina, ferns, bamboo, Tahitian chestnut or *mape,* wild banana or *fei, purau,* pandanus.

fauna
Rather poor. Only amongst the birds there a several interesting indigenous species: white-tail tropicbird, reef heron, grey duck, crested or sw tern, Tahiti lorikeet and the very common Indi mynah.
Amongst the insects: cockroaches, ants, mud daub wasps, bees, spiders, flies and mosquitoes. A lar scolopendra, the centipede, has a very painful stin There are no reptiles, except small lizards.
On the other hand, the sea fauna is very rich, both the lagoon and in the open sea: more than 30 species of fish; shell-fish such as crabs, lobsters a shrimps; also oysters, mother-of-pearl, clams, et Tides are regular: low at 6 o'clock am and pm; hi at 12 o'clock am and pm. These are solar tides a of limited movement.

history
The inhabitants of French Polynesia are descendan of the Maori migrations in the first century A.I When the Europeans arrived in the XVI and XV centuries, they found an organized and well-est blished society in Polynesia. Several expedition were necessary to discover all the islands. Tahiti w visited for the first time in 1767 by Wallis; then I Bougainville in 1768, Cook in 1769 and Bligh 1788. The latter became famous because of th mutiny on the "Bounty".
Cook also discovered the Leeward Islands and certa islands of the Tuamotu archipelago. The Marquesa were discovered by the Spaniards in 1595; then we visited by Cook in 1774 and by Ingraham in 179 The Australs were gradually discovered first by Coc in 1768, then by Gayangos, Varela and Vancouve Until 1880 Tahiti was governed by the Poma

ynasty. It then became a French colony, including
the neighbouring islands. In 1957 French Polynesia
acquired the status of a French overseas territory.

population

137,382 inhabitants in French Polynesia. 74% live
in the Windward Islands and over 50% of these on
Tahiti itself. Polynesian Maoris represent 75% of
the population. Chinese represent 7%, Europeans
.6%, Half-Europeans 7.2%, Half-Chinese 0.9% and
others 1.3%.

religion

Two religions represent the vast majority: Protestants
0% and Catholics 35%. Mormons, 7th Day Adven-
sts and Jehovah's Witnesses 15%.

language

French and Tahitian are the official languages. Pua-
motu, Marquesan and Cantonese are also spoken.
English is spoken in hotels, restaurants, shops, etc.

economy

Mainly based on fishing, agriculture and tourism.
Since the establishment of the C.E.P. in 1960, due
to the French nuclear tests, Polynesian economy has
undergone a great change. Through taxes, the C.E.P.
has payed large sums of money on imported mer-
chandise sent to Hao, Mururoa and Fangataufa. The
C.E.P. and the C.E.A. have also given work to many.
This economic boom has brought with it a frantic
consumer society that has sent prices sky-rocketing.
The artificial prosperity created by the C.E.P. is now
ending. The problems incurred in finding an economic
balance in order to avoid total dependance on the
outside world have resulted in much hardship. A new
economy based on tourism, agriculture and fishing is
now being encouraged.

administration and political organization

A new statute came into effect on July 12 1977 and
the territory of French Polynesia is now administered
by both a High Commissioner of the Republic and the
Territorial Service. The latter comprises: a Government Council which meets once a week and which is
made up of the High Commissioner, as President, a
Vice-President and 6 other members; a Territorial
Assembly of 30 elected members with two sessions
a year, and lastly, an advisory Committee for Social
and Economic Affairs. The Territorial Assembly and
Government Counsel look after local affairs. The
whole territory is divided into 5 administrative districts.

how to get there

By plane: 6 international Airlines fly to French Polynesia: U.T.A., Qantas, Air New Zealand, Lan Chile, Air Pacific and S.P.I.A. from Honolulu.

The international airport is at Faaa, 5 km from Papeete.

By ship: no ocean liners call here regularly.

entry-formalities

Immigration officials: a passport and sometimes a visa is neaded for all except French citizens, who only need their identity card. An American visa is needed for those stopping over in the U.S.A. except if in transit. A return or continuation ticket is also required, or a deposit equivalent to the price of a return ticket. A dispensation of this requirement might be obtained. *Customs:* up to 200 cigarettes or 50 cigars and 2 litres alcoholic beverage may be brought in.

what to wear

No formalities; light cotton clothes and swimsuits. Perhaps also a cardigan and a light raincoat. Everything can be bought in Papeete, but prices are rather high.

exchange rates

Monetary units is the Pacific franc (CFP). 1 French franc = 18,18 CFP. The exchange rate for foreign currencies will very with the fluctuation of the French Franc to which the French Pacific Franc is tied.

news media

There is the government Radio/Television station RF with colour television daily from 3.30 to 10.00 pm to Tahi Moorea and the Leewards islands, plus two private rad stations, RTA and FM 100.

Two daily newspaper in French "La Dépêche" and "Le Nouvelles"; plus a complimentary English language wee ly publication, "Tahiti Sunpress".

International newspapers and magazines arrive weekly t air mail.

health

There is one hospital in Tahiti at Mamao, two clinics: Ca della and Paofai, and one medical institute: Mallardé, fc tropical disease research. There are also private doctor dentists and chemists.

The other islands have at least a surgery, with a doct and a nurse.

The most common hazards are dengue, fish poisonin cutting oneself on the coral, stonefish stings.

travelling

Land transportation consists of: the "truck" —Tahitia bus typical and inexpensive; taxis, with the price-lis established by the government shown in each car hire cars in Tahiti, Moorea, Bora Bora, Raiatea Huahine and Rangiroa.

Air Polynesia (offices in Papeete) links the islands, an so do several ferries. From Tahiti there are th following flights: Moorea in 7 min (15 km); Huahin in 40 min (170 km); Raiatea in 45 min (220 km) Bora Bora in 50 min no stops and 1 hour 10 mi stopping at Raiatea (260 km); Maupiti in 20 min from Bora Bora (315 km); Rangiroa in 1 hour (350 km) Manihi in 2 hours 40 min stopping at Rangiro (520 km); Tubuai in 1 hour 50 (670 km); Uahuk

...d Hivaoa (Marquesas) in 7 hours 50 min stopping
Rangiroa and Manihi.
...r Tahiti flies to Moorea from Tahiti every 20 min.
...aggage allowance is 10 kg.

...cal crafts
...teresting objects to buy: sculptures in wood *(tiki, ...nete...),* nacres, shells and shelljewelry, wicker-
...ork (hats, baskets, mats...) pareu material, clothes
...ade of hand-printed material, *tifaifai* (kind of
...atchwork: cushion-covers and bedspreads), *tapa*
...ainted bark), etc.

...urist information
...e tourist bureau (Office du Tourisme) operates at
...aa Airport and on the Pomare boulevard, Papeete.
...el. 296.26. open throughout the week from 7:30 a.m.
... 5 p.m., and on Saturdays from 9 a.m. to 4 p.m.

...nts
... The best time to visit Polynesia is from May to
...ctober.
... Tap water is fit for drinking.
... Alter. current (60 per.) is of 110 or 220 volts.
... Tipping is against the rules of hospitality.
... Shops are open from 7.30 to 11.30 a.m. and from
...to 5 p.m.
... Prices are official: no bargaining.
... Central post office is in Papeete. There are post
...fices on almost all the other islands. Telephone
...tween Tahiti, Moorea, Raiatea, Huahine, Bora Bora is
...tomatic. Communications between the other islands is
...' radiotelephone. Tahiti is linked by satellite to the inter-
...tional telephone system and may now be dialled direct.

tahiti

Tahiti lies in the South Pacific halfway between
Australia and the U.S.A. It is the main island of
French Polynesia, covering 1,042 km². Tahiti is a
volcanic island, very fertile, formed by two volcanoes
united by an isthmus. It is surrounded by coral reefs
that protect the lagoons. The highest mountain is
Mount Orohena, 2,234 m. (See map on end-paper pages)

population
95,604 people live in Tahiti, 23,453 of which live
in Papeete. The Tahitians are known for their extreme
kindness, good will and natural gaiety.

hotels
De luxe :
Beachcomber (Travelodge), Faaa, B.P. 364 -
tel. 251.10
Maeva Beach, Punaauia, B.P. 6008 - tel. 280.42.
Tahara'a, Arue, B.P. 1015 - tel. 811.22.
Grade A :
Holiday Inn, Vallée de Tipaerui, B.P. 32 -
tel. 267.67.
Kon Tiki, Papeete, B.P. 111 - tel. 295.99.
Royal Papeete, Papeete, B.P. 919 - tel. 201.29.
Royal Tahitien, Pirae, B.P. 5001 - tel. 281.13.
Grade B :
Princesse Heiata, Pirae, B.P. 497 - tel. 281.05.
Hotel Tahiti, Papeete, B.P. 416 - tel. 295.50.
Te Puna Bel Air, Faaa, B.P. 354 - tel. 282.24.
Hotels on the circle island tour :
Le Petit Mousse, Papara, B.P. 32 tel. 742.07.

restaurants

Hotel restaurants have not been included in the following list.

Papeete and surroundings:

French restaurants:

Acajou, bd Pomare, Fare Tony, tel. 287.58.
Auberge Landaise, seafront, tel. 377.14.
Le Belvédère, route de Fare Rau Ape, Pirae, tel. 273.44.
Le Bistrot du Port, seafront, Papeete, tel. 255.09.
Le Bougainville, rue Tepano-Jaussen, tel. 299.53
Changuy, rue des Remparts, tel. 287.76.
La Chaumière, Pamatai, tel. 282.52.
La Crémaillère, chemin de Patutoa, tel. 209.15.
Au Col Bleu, grill-room, bd Pomare, tel. 296.78.
Le Fautaua, Hamuta, Pirae, tel. 274.00.
La Frégate, Pont de l'Est, tel. 203.59.
Le Lion d'Or, rue Afarerii, Pirae, tel. 266.50.
Le Madrepore, Vaima Center, tel. 243.23.
Manava, avenue Bruat, Papeete, tel. 202.91.
Moana Iti, bd Pomare, Paofai, tel. 298.85.
La Petite Auberge, Pont de 1'Est, tel. 206.13.
Le Steak House, avenue du Prince Hinoi, Papeete, tel. 251.55.
Vaima, cafe and restaurant, Vaima Center, tel. 297.45.

Chinese restaurants:

Dahlia, Arue, route de Ceinture, tel. 259.87.
Le Dragon d'Or, rue Colette, tel. 296.12.
Liou Foung, avenue du Prince-Hinoi, tel. 209.82.
Le Mandarin, rue des Ecoles, tel. 299.03.
Jade Palace, Vaima Center, tel. 202.19.
Pitate Mamao, avenue G. Clemenceau, tel. 286.94.
La soupe Chinoise, rue Gauguin, tel. 297.48.
Te Hoa, Pirae, tel. 206.91.
Waikiki, rue A. Leboucher, tel. 295.27.

other restaurants:

La Pizzeria, italian food, on the seafront, tel. 298.30.
Lou Pescadou, pizzeria, rue Cardella, tel. 374.26.
La Baie d'Along, vietnamese, avenue du Prince Hinoi, Papeete, tel. 205.35.

Restaurants on the circle island tour:

Auberge du Pacifique, Punaauia, tel. 821.09.
Baie des Pêcheurs, Punaauia, tel. 822.95.
Coco's, Punaauia, tel. 821.08.
Nahiti Nui, Mahina, tel. 815.49.
Le Petit Mousse, Papara, tel. 742.07.
Nuutere, relais Chapiteau, Papara, tel. 741.15.
Restaurant du Musée Gauguin, Papeari, tel. 713.80.
Le Rotui, Faaone, tel. 714.44.
Te Moana, Lagoonarium, Punaauia, tel. 829.91.
Taiarapu, Taravao, tel. 711.51.
Vahine Moea, Papara, tel. 741.70.
Vahoata, Mataeia, tel. 742.44.

rent-a-car

Rates are according to mileage or on a daily basis and vary depending on the type of car rented.
The main rent-a-car agencies are:
André, near Hotel Kon Tiki, tel. 294.04.
Avis, rue Charles-Vienot, tel. 296.49.
Europcar, Bd Pomare, tel. 246.16.
Henry, Pirae, tel. 270.81.
Hertz, rue Cdt-Destremeau, tel. 204.71.
Pacificar, rue des remparts, tel. 243.64.
Polynesian Rental, Airport, tel. 307.70.
Robert, Bd Pomare, tel. 297.20.
Toyota rent a car, Mamao, tel. 298.19.
T.T.T., Tipaerui Valley, tel. 276.39.

nt-a-boat (for fishing or cruising).
ahiti Yachting, tel. 278.03.
aura Club (deep sea fishing), tel. 289.10.
or deep sea fishing or chartered trips, contact the yachts
n the quayside, or ask in a travel agency.
ahiti Cruising Club, Place Notre Dame, tel. 268.89.

ports
port clubs and associations abound in Tahiti.
ercle Equestre de Pirae, tel. 270.41.
ssociation Hippique, Hippodrome, Pirae,
l. 281.12.
Jay pigeon shooting, Hotel Tahara'a, tel. **811.22**.
ennis Club, Fautaua Stadium, tel. 200.59.
lost hotels have tennis courts.
olf Club, Atimaono, Mataiea **tel. 742.41**.
olf — Hotel Tahara'a, tel. 811.23.
ountain climbing:
lub Alpin (M. Jay), Arue, tel. 810.59.
éro-Club — Faaa International Airport,
l. 280.61.
arachute Club, Faaa Airport, tel. 280.61.
ridge Club, Hotel Maeva Beach, tel. 280.42.
owling — Arue, P.K.5,6, tel. 293.26.
ater sports are very varied and facilities exist
hotels as well as in sport clubs.
eep sea fishing, Haura Club, tel. 289.10.
nderwater Fishing Club, tel. 281.54.
ahiti Yacht Club, P.K. 4, Arue, tel. 278.03.
urf Club, tel. 297.80.
ahiti Aquatic, Hotel Maeva Beach, tel. 280.42.
xtension 0951).
ahiti Actinautic, **Hotel Beachcomber, tel. 251.10.**
wimming pool, Tipaerui, tel. 289.24.
ubs:

Rotary Club, Hotel Maeva Beach, tel. 280.42.
Lion's Club, c/o Holiday Inn, tel. 267.67.

celebrations
New year's day - March 5: Arrival of the Gospel
celebrations - Easter Friday to Monday - May 1st -
Ascension Day - Whit Monday - July 14 (French
national holiday) - All Saints - Armistice Day -
Christmas.
The most important celebration is the Tiurai, during
the week of July 14, which lasts at least two weeks.
Dancing contests, canoe races, horse races, javelin-
throwing contests, etc.
Other important celebrations: *Chinese New Year,*
Night of the Guitar, Ball of Tahiti in Times Gone By,
Night of the Vahine and Tiare Day.

nightlife
Local groups provide the music in hotel discothèques.
Most hotels put on shows with traditional Tahitian
dancing.
Here are a selection of bars and nightclubs in Papeete:
Le Bounty Club, discothèque, Rue des Ecoles,
tel. 293.00.
La Cave Royal Papeete, Hotel Royal Papeete,
tel. 201.29.
Le Café de Paris, Hotel Maeva, tel. 280.42.
Mayana Club, Bruat Centre, tel. 382.29.
Le Pitate and Le Seven Seas (upstairs), Avenue Bruat,
tel. 283.04.
Le Roll's Club, Vaima Center, tel. 262.41.
Le Tiki Room, Holiday Inn, tel. 267.67.
Le Piano Bar, Rue des Ecoles, tel. 288.24.
La Princesse Heiata, Pirae, tel. 281.05.

Le Whisky à gogo, (discothèque), Bd Pomare, tel. 273.05.
Le Zizou Bar, Bd Pomare, tel. 207.55.

some of the main cinemas
Drive in Punaauia, near Maeva Beach.
Drive in Arue, 2 kilometers from Papeete.
Mamao Palace, Mamao.
Le Concorde 1 and 2, Vaima Center.
Le Liberty, Rue du Maréchal-Foch.
Hollywood I and 2, Fare Tony.
There is also a Cultural Center at Paofai, which has a cineclub, theatre, library and dance school.

museums
Gauguin Museum, tel. 710.58, open every day from 9 a.m. to 5 p.m.
Museum of Tahiti and its Islands, Pointe des Pêcheurs, Punaauia, tel 834.76. Open from Tuesday to Sunday from 8 a.m. to 5 p.m.
Museum of the Discovery, Pointe Vénus, tel. 812.20. Open every day from 9 a.m. to 12 a.m.

art galleries
Winkler Laurent (primitive art), rue Jeanne d'Arc, tel. 292.52.
Galerie Noa Noa (oriental), bd Pomare, tel. 273.47.
Galerie Vaite, Vaima Center, tel. 246.80.
Tahiti Art - Matamua, seafront, tel. 297.43.
Galerie Vaimantic, Vaima Center, tel. 368.96.

tours and excursions
Travel agencies and tour operators:
Manureva Tours, B.P. 1745, Papeete, tel. 272.58.

Pacific Travel, B.P. 605, Papeete, tel. 293.85.
Tahiti Nui, B.P. 718, Papeete, tel. 204.91.
Tahiti Poroi, B.P. 83, Papeete, tel. 200.70.
Tahiti Voyages, B.P. 485, Papeete, tel. 203.63.
Tahiti Tours, B.P. 627, Papeete, tel. 278.70
Voyagence Tahiti, B.P. 131, Papeete, tel. 249.43.
Vahine Tahiti Travel, B.P. 1699, tel. 244.83.

possible excursions
A visit of Papeete: governor's residence - Quee Marau's house - site of the ex-British Consulate Paofai Temple - Bougainville Park - Papeete sea-front - industrial zone of Fare Ute - Motu Uta wharf.
A tour of the lagoon in a glass bottom boat.
A tama'ara'a (Tahitian meal cooked underground) organized either by an agency or by a hotel.
The Lagoonarium of Tahiti is well worth a visit - Punaauia, P.K. 11,5 tel. 829.91.

circle island tour going east
2.5 km: Bain Loti - Fautaua river.
4.7 km: Tomb of King Pomare V.
5.4 km: James Norman Hall's house.
8.1 km: Taharaa Hill and Hotel.
11 km: Point Venus - Matavai Bay.
11.7 km: Mahina, Towards the right, two roads into the mountains. View of the sea.
13.2 km: Orofara leper village.
17.1 km: Papenoo valley.
22 km: Arahoho blow hole.
22.5 km: Fa'arumai valley waterfalls.
37.6 km: Boungainville's anchorage.
39 km: Splendid view of the peninsula.
41.8 km: Fa'atautia waterfalls.
49.2 km: Rotui restaurant.
53 km: Taravao village.

.6 km: Mountain road towards a splendid view point.
6.5/18 km: Village, bay and river of Tautira, where
obert Louis Stevenson lived.
eturn to Taravao.
.3 km: Zane Grey's territory.
.5 km: Natural harbor - legendary hero Maui is said
o have left his footprints on the reef.
8 km: Village of Teahuupoo, return to Taravao.

ircle island tour going west

5 km: Robert Keable's house.
1.6 km: Harrison W. Smith's botanical gardens and
ie Gauguin Museum.
0 km: Gauguin Museum's restaurant.
8 km: Road to Lake Vaihiria.
6.5 km: Village where Gauguin lived from 1891 to
893.
4 km: Rupert Brooke's haven.
1 km: Atimaono golf course.
9.2 km: Ruins of the great *marae* Mahaitea.
6 km: Andersonville memorial at Papara.
8.5 km: Paroa cave.
2.5 km: *Marae* in the Arahurahu valley.
2.6 km: A school indicated by the sign "2+2=4".
ear the site where Gauguin once lived.
.5 km: Faaa international airport.
.5 km: Mountain road - view of Papeete.

ıoorea

ıoorea is some 17 km to the north-west of Tahiti.

opulation

,788 inhabitants throughout the 5 principal areas:
eavaro, Papetoai, Paopao, Afareaitu and Haapiti.

access

By sea: leaving from Papeete - Moorea quay every
day between 9 and 9.30 a.m. The trip takes slightly
over 1 hour. The ferries are the following:
— *Keke III,* stopping at Hotels Bali Hai, Aimeo and
Paopao village. Tel. 280.60.
— *Maire,* stopping at Paopao and Vaiare Bay. Tel. 810.17.
— *Tamarii Moorea* (Afareaitu, Vaiare Bay). Tel. 293.97.
— *The Moorea Ferry.* Tel. 373.64.
By plane: the flight takes 7 min. Air Tahiti has flights
every 25 min.

hotels

Club Bali Hai - B.P. 627, Papeete, Tel. 613.68.
Bali Hai Moorea - B.P. 415, Papeete, Tel. 613.59.
Cable address: Bali Hai Moorea
Hotel Captain Cook's Bay - Haapiti, tel. 610.60.
Club Méditerranée Village - B.P. 575, Papeete,
tel. 296.99. Cable address: Mediclub Papeete.
Kia Ora Village — B.P. 706, Papeete, tel. 286.72 and
612.90.
Moorea Lagon, tel. 614.68. Cable address: Morlagon
Papeete.
Moorea Village — Fare Gendron, Haapiti, Moorea,
tel. 610.02.
Résidence Les Tipaniers - Haapiti, Moorea,
tel. 612.67.
Village Club Kaveka -Pao Pao, Moorea, Tel. 610.60.

other places to stay while in Moorea

Albert Haring has 10 houses facing the mountains in
the village of Pao Pao, tel. 612.76. Full address:
Albert Haring, Pao Pao, Moorea, French Polynesia.
Hotel Chez Pauline — small traditional inn with restaurant. Address: Mme Teariki Afareaitu, Moorea, tel.
611.26.

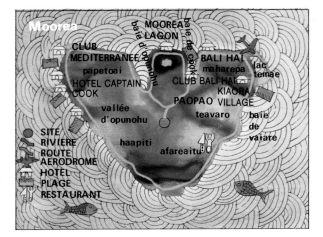

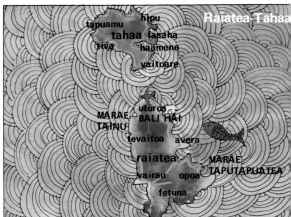

Chez Cordier — 8 bungalows, 7 of which are beside the sea. Address: M. Cordier Maharepa, Tiaia, Moorea, tel. 670.35.
Marcel Jamet has 8 beachfront bungalows for rent at Haapiti, Tel. 614.36.
Chez Taae — seaside house. Address: René Taae Afareaitu, Moorea, tel. 610.69.

restaurants:
Chez Coco — Papetoai, French and Chinese food, with a Tahitian oven on Sundays, tel. 610.03.
Fare Manava — Cook's Bay Pao Pao. French cuisine. tel. 614.24.
L'Aquarium — Maharepe, tel. 613.54.
Restaurant Hakka — Maharepa, tel. 612.19.
L'Escargot — Haapiti, tel. 614.09.
Restaurant Hoy Yong — Paopao, tel. 610.29.
Restaurant Temae — Moorea airport. Tel. 614.39.
Chez Billy — *Tama'ara'a.* Tahitian specialities. Ring Billy Ruta, tel. 612.54.

transportation
Taxi or bus: from hotels to airport and vice-versa.
Truck: upon arrival of ferries and other ships.

rent-a-car
Billy Tours, in front of Club Méditerranée, tel. 611.63.
Moorea Rent-a-Car, Moorea airport, tel. 614.12.
Avis Rent-a-Car, Hotel Kia Ora, tel. 610.46.

sports
The hotels offer all sorts of water sports: water-skiing, diving, etc. Bicycles can be rented to visit the island.

Horse riding at *Moorea Ranch,* Haapiti, tel. 613.10 The hotels also organize picnics and excursions.

excursions
The island tour is possible by car, as there are 60 kr of good roads.
What must be seen:
— Cook's Bay.
— Opunohu Bay.
— Vaiare Bay and Pierced Mountain.
— Churches and temples, namely: the octagona temple of Papetoai - the Catholic mission c Haapiti with its two square towers - the Catholi mission of Paopao with a nativity by Heymann.
— The *marae:* at Nuurua, at Maatea, Afareaitu an Titiroa near the school of agriculture.
— The crater road. It starts from the village of Paopac crosses the pineapple plantations and arrives at viewpoint from which a splendid view of both th bay of Cook and of Opunohu can be observec separated by Mount Rotui. The road descend towards Opunohu Bay crossing the agricultura college.

raiatea

It is the second largest island in the Society arch pelago, 238 km², in the shape of a triangle. Th highest moutain is the Temehani, 1,033 m. Raiate is encircled by the same lagoon as Tahaa, th neighbouring island.

population
The largest population in the Leeward Islands

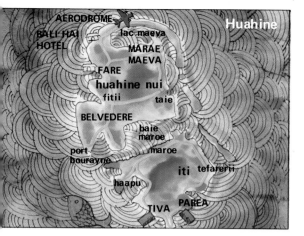

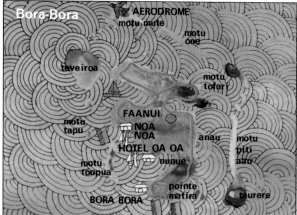

,885 inhabitants of which 2,517 live in Uturoa, a sort of small capital with a port, an airport, a school, a hospital, government offices and several shops.

ccess

y plane: Air Polynesia flies several times a day etween Raiatea and Papeete. The direct flight is 5 min., stopping at Huahine, 65 min.
y ship: every **Monday** at 7 p.m. two ferries leave apeete stopping at Huahine and Raiatea—the *emehani* (tel. 298.83) and the *Taporo IV* (tel. 263.93)

ansportation

ruck: twice a day from Uturoa to the other villages nd back (Opoa, Avera, Tevaitoa, Fetuna and Vaiaau). lso from the airport to Uturoa and Bali Hai Hotel.
axi: airport, Uturoa and Bali Hai Hotel.

nt-a-car

lr. Guirouard, Motu Tapu Garage, Uturoa, tel. 633.09.

nt-a-boat

- *Ah Tchoung:* BP 91, opposite Tiare Cinema.

ccommodation

otel Bali Hai — Uturoa, tel. 631.49. Telegraphs: Bali ai Raiatea.
otel Vairahi - tel. 630.71

staurants

downtown Uturoa: *Jade garden*, Chinese; *Le Motu*, ench and sea food; *Te Orama*, *Chez Remy*, *Le laraamu*, chinese and tahitian cooking.
l these restaurants are near the marketplace.

excursions

The circle island tour can be made by car, except the southern coast. The principal sights are: the visit to a "fare" at which an *umuti* or "fire dance" is done by the people of Apooiti village. It is opposite the Bali Hai Hotel in Tupua bay. The visit to the most famous *marae* in Polynesia, the Taputapuatea *marae* (meaning "extended and very sacred"), one of the highlights of ancient Maori civilisation. The *marae* of Tainuu is at Tevaitoa, on the west coast. Also certain *marae* ruins on mount Toomaru (1,017 m).
The *Bali Hai Hotel* organizes excursions by mini-bus and also on the lagoon by speed-boats. It offers all sorts of sports: water-skiing, under-water diving, under-water fishing, horse-riding, tennis and sailing at the Uturoa Yacht Club.
There are both telephone and television on the island.

tahaa

Tahaa faces Raiatea in the same lagoon. It is a circular island, covering 82 km². Its highest peaks are Mount Ohiri (590 m) and Mount Purauti (550 m). The southern coast has several deep bays.

population

With a total population of 3,513 inhabitants, Tahaa is divided into 8 districts: Hipu, Niua, Tapuamu, Iripau, Ruutia, Vaitoare, Haamene and Faaaha. The main village is Patio, which is the furthest from Raiatea.

access
Only by boat. A ship leaves from Uturoa every Wednesday and Friday at 12.30 a.m. It arrives at Vaitoare and returns to Uturoa on the same days at 3 p.m.

accomodation
Between the villages of Tapuamu and Tiva: *Tahaa village* offers 9 bungalows on the waterfront. Contact M. Petit Tetuanui, Tapuamu, Tiva, île de Tahaa.

excursions
In Vaitoare is the tomb of Rarahu, the Tahitian girl described in *The Marriage of Loti* (1882) by the French writer Pierre Loti. To visit the island, a road leads from Hipu to Tiva and as far as Hurepiti Bay. To continue one must follow a small path. On the mountain the rocks have different names according to the animals or things they ressemble. The island tour can be made by boat, visiting the beautiful bays of Hurepiti, Apu, Haamene and Faaaha. See M. Petit Tetuanui (above) to rent a boat.

---

tetiaora

Tetiaroa is an atoll 47 km north of Tahiti, formed by several coral islets surrounded by a reef. There is a small pass on the northwest border that only small boats can use. The island used to belong to the royal Pomare family and today it is the property of actor Marlon Brando who has set up a tourist center: *Tetiaroa Village.*

access
By boat: certain ferries stop at times to unload carg and passengers.
By plane: There are 3 flights a week from Tahiti Wednesdays, Saturdays and Sundays. The fligh takes 20 minutes.

accommodation
Tetiaroa Village is built in the Polynesian style. Fo reservations, write to Tetiaroa Village, B.P. 2418 Papeete, Tahiti. Cable address: Tetiaroa Papeete Tel. 813.02.

---

huahine

Huahine lies 130 km to the north-west of Papeet and 32 km to the east of Raiatea. It is formed by two islands: Huahine Nui (large Huahine) whose highes peak is Mount Turi (669 m) and Huahine Iti (smal Huahine) whose highest peak is Mount Puhaere (462 m). The entire surface is 74 km².

population
There are 3,140 inhabitants in Huahine. The islan is divided into 8 sections, 4 in Huahine Nui (Fare, th capital, with post office, police station and surgery Fitii, Faie and Maeva) and 4 in Huahine Iti (Haapu Parea, Tefarerii, Maroe).

access
By boat: Two ferries leave from Papeete every Monda at 7 p.m.: the Taporo IV and the Temehani.
By plane: There are 14 flights a week from Tahiti b Air Polynesia. The flight takes 40 minutes.

transportation

here is a road from Maeva to Parea, passing by Fare,
itii and Haapu. There are both taxis and trucks at
are, Parea and Airport.

ent-a-car: Francois Rent-a-Car. Address: Francois
efoc, Village de Fare Huahine, tel. 76.
vis Rent-a-Car, Bali Hai Hotel, tel. 34.
he island tour can be made either by taxi or by mini-
us.

accommodation

otel Bali Hai, Fare, Cable address: Bali Hai Huahine.
otel Huahine, Fare. Twelve rooms with showers.
ooms with showers.
ension Enite, downtown Fare.
hez Lorina, downtown Fare.
hez Ah Foussan, Fare. 4 rooms with showers. No
estaurant.
otel Bellevue, Maroe. 8 rooms.

accommodation in private homes

here are two possibilities in Parea: with Urua Viri
Pension Mémé), accommodation for 10 to 15 people.
ome cooking. Address: M. Urua Viri, Tavana
area, Huahine; with Albert Temeharo, with 7 rooms
nd able to accommodate 14 people. Home cooking.
rite to: M. Albert Temeharo, Parea, Huahine.

restaurants

are Haapua (snackbar). Fare, Huahine.
hez Mama Peni (café-restaurant), on the seafront at
are, Huahine.

excursions

There is a road all around Huahine Iti and almost all
around Huahine Nui. Towards Parea, the road runs
along the coast and also through vanilla plantations
in the mountains. After Fitii there is a viewpoint from
which one can admire, on one side Maroe Bay and on
the other Bourayne port. A one hundred meter long
bridge unites both islands. On Huahine Iti the road
runs along the lagoon and goes through the villages of
Maroe, Tefarerii and Parea. There are beautiful white
sand beaches on Tiva and Haapu peninsulas.
Towards the airport, the road runs beside Maeva
Lake. A little before the village of Maeva, it
runs beside an important archaeological site with
several *marae;* amongst these, the famous Maununu
marae. The old, picturesque village on stilts was built
at the foot of Maua Tapu, the sacred mountain
(429 m). The road ends at Faie but a path reaches the
viewpoint between Fitii and Parea. Another path runs
along the coast, crossing the islet between the ocean
and Lake Maeva, through coconut groves and watermelon and melon plantations, till it reaches the airport
and Fare.
By boat, the island tour offers the following sights:
the west coast after *Bali Hai Hotel,* passing by the
Bays of Haapu, Parea, Tefarerii, Maroe and Bourayne
Port; visit to Anini *marae* and Avea beach; excursions
to the *motu* of Araa and Topatii.

bora bora

Bora Bora lies 270 km north-west of Tahiti. The main
island is surrounded by a barrier reef and several islets.
There is only one pass that can be used to cross into

the lagoon and the airport is built on a *motu*. Bora Bora covers 38 km² and its highest peak is Mount Otemanu (727 m).

population
There are 2,572 inhabitants on the island. The principal village is Vaitape, with the administrator's residence, the post office, police station, surgery and port.

access
By boat: two ferries leave from Tahiti alternatively every week: the *Temehani* and the *Taporo IV*. *By plane:* 3 to 5 flights a day from Tahiti, by Air Polynesia. Either 70 minute flight, stopping at Huahine and Raiatea; or 50 minute flight without stopovers.

accommodation
Hotel Bora Bora — Cable address: Borhotel Bora Bora. *Le Club Méditerranée*, Vaitape — Cable address: Mediclub Papeete. *Hotel Oa-Oa*, Vaitape: Family style — Reservations: Tahiti Tours: B.P. 627, Papeete, Tahiti. *Hotel Marara*, Anau owner: Dino de Laurentis. *Hotel Marina*, Motu Mute: 45 rooms. *Bloody Mary's* bungalows, Nunue: tahitian style. *Bora Bora Yacht Club*, Vaitape: 3 bungalows. *Altex bungalows*, Pointe Matira: 10 bungalows on the lagoon - Reservations: John Lee c/o Chaussures Altex, B. P. 187, Papeete.

rent-a-car
Bora Bora Tours Rent-a-Car. Vaitape village.
Otemanu Rent-a-Car. Vaitape.
Bicycles and motorcycles can also be rented. Both agencies organize minibus excursions round the island.

rent-a-boat
Moana Adventure Tours. Owner Erwin Christian can offer you: glass-bottom boat, excursions on the reef, picnic on an island, water-skiing, diving.

things to do
All sorts of nautical sports are practised: canoe and speedboat excursions, deepwater diving, night-fishing in the lagoon, shell collecting. A traditional stone fishing excursion can be organized by the chief of Vaitape village, upon request.
The island tour takes you along 32 kms of coral road beside the lagoon. Visit the tomb of French navigator Alain Gerbault in Vaitape, on the site of an ancient *marae*.
Mountain climbing is possible on Mt. Pahia (661 m). The climb takes 3 hours. Visit Motu-Toopua and Motu-Tapu Islands, tour the island by boat (2 to 4 hours) and see the Taianapa *marae* near Faanui village (km 26).

maupiti

Maupiti lies 37 km west of Bora-Bora. It has a total circumference of 9.6 km and its highest point reaches 372 m. It has a surface of 25 km² and is surrounded by a barrier reef.

population
710 inhabitants. There used to be 9 administrative centers; only two remain today—Vaiea and Farauru. The port, school, surgery and town hall are at Farauru.

access
By boat: service not guaranteed between Raiatea and Maupiti.

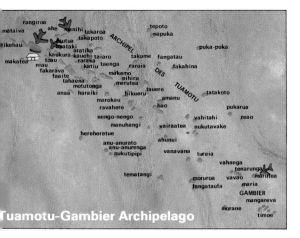

Tuamotu-Gambier Archipelago

ferry, the *Kia Ora,* leaves Papeete every two weeks.
by plane: 3 weekly flights from Tahiti by Air Polynesia.
1h 10 min. stopping at Raiatea and Bora-Bora.

accommodation
Raioho (9 rooms, bar and restaurant). Address:
Mr. Raioho Teroro, Maupiti, Leeward Islands.
Augustina Tavaearii has accommodation and can rent
you bicycles and a boat.
Frida Tuheiava, Anna Tinorua and *Teha Teupoohuita* offer
rooms and meals.
Motel Avira, Hu'apiti islet and Vilna Tavaearu, Tiapaa islet.

excursions
There is a new road around the island, but it is
well worth taking the old coastal path, starting
from Vaiea village, which takes about 3 hours. On
Rae'oa motu, the oldest archaeological site in the
Leeward Islands can be visited. There are also marae
platforms, stone walls and dolmens to be seen on the
island, with white sand beaches and islets to visit.

local crafts
Maupiti used to be well known for its crafts in stone
and wood. Today the local craft is mainly mother-of-
pearl fish-hooks. There are 7 different kinds of
mother-of-pearl, used for the 7 kinds of fish-hook—one
for each kind of fishing. These are still used today.

tuamotu-gambier archipelago

The Tuamotu-Gambier archipelago is the largest in
French Polynesia, formed by 84 islands that lie along
a strip 2,300 km long and 400 to 500 km wide. The
total land surface is 922 km², spread out over
20,000 km² of ocean. The principal island is
Rangiroa. With the exception of Makatea, all the
islands are low and of coral origin (atolls).

population
The Tuamotu islands are not densely populated. Of
the 84 islands, only 41 are inhabited. The population
is 8,496 — only 7% of the total population of French
Polynesia. The largest number live in Rangiroa:
1,427 inhabitants.

access
By plane: Air Polynesia flies to 8 atolls in the Tuamotu;
there are flights to Rangiroa (65 min.) 6 days a week
(except Tuesdays). Wednesdays, Fridays and Sundays
connections with Manihi; only on Fridays connections with Tikehau. Once a week, on Friday, there is a
flight from Papeete to Kaukura, apataki, Fakarava,
Takapoto returning the same day. There are weekly
flights to Anaa and Makemo, and once a week (Friday) connections with Mataiva. For further information
contact Air Polynesia 224.44.
By boat: Several ferries leave Papeete for the Tuamotu
Islands. Tickets are generally bought aboard and often
meals are not served. The trip Papeete/Rangiroa takes
about 20 hours. For exact dates of departure, phone the
owners of the ferries:—
Saint-Corentin — tel. 2.91.69.
Saint Xavier Maris Stella — tel. 2.84.55.
Tamarii Tikehau — tel. 2.52.57.
There are atomic centers in Mururoa and Fangataufa,
and a C.E.P. base in Hao. These atolls have ports and airports, but being military bases, access is forbidden to
unauthorized civilians.

accommodation
At Rangiroa:

Between Avatoru and Tiputa villages: *Hotel Kia Ora Village.* Deluxe, with 25 Polynesian bungalows. Address: B.P. 706, Papeete — Tahiti. Tel. 286.72.
Avatoru village: *Tavita Ami has 5 bungalows and 4 large rooms (can lodge 30 people). Boats for rent. Tel. Papeete 813.05.* Pension Fareaa: 11 bungalows.
At Manihi:
Kaina Village Hotel. Tel. papeete 275.53. 16 Polynesian bungalows with restaurant and water sports. Manager: Coco Chaze. Mme Rei Estall has room for 30 people, full board possible. Tel. 243.73 or 288.44 (Papeete).
Things to do in Manihi: walks on the reef, visits to the *motu,* visits to the pearl and fish farms, underwater fishing.
On the motu (coral islets):
Motu Teavatia, 15 km from avatoru, whitesand beach, 3 bungalows.
Motu Tatiavao, 1 hour by boat from Tiputa, 5 tahitians bungalows.
Motu Avea, 1 hours by boat from Tiputa, 1 house for around 15 persons.
Motu Matatahi, Hotel Roonui Village, 10 bungalows.
Motu Mahuta, Village sans souci, 15 bungalows.

gambier archipelago

The Gambier Islands are different from the Tuamotu: they include 4 high islands and a few atolls. They lie to the south of the Tuamotu. The principal island, Mangareva, reaches its highest point at 435 m. The population is not numerous: some 556 inhabitants in Rikitea, the capital. Air Polynesia has two monthly flights from Papeete. Ferries call from time to time and the C.E.P. has built a landing strip, which is used by air companies upon request. Agriculture, the copra industry, fishing and pearl culture are the main livelihoods of the inhabitants.

marquesas archipelago

The Marquesas lie 1,500 km north-east of Tahiti. They form two groups, 14 islands covering 1,275 km². The two groups are: in the north, Nukuhiva, Uauka and Uapou; in the south, Hivaoa, Tahuata and Fatuhiva.
They are high, craggy islands: their peaks rise to over 1,000 m and their coasts are not protected by barrier reefs.

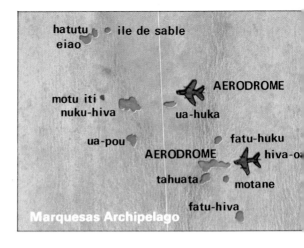

Marquesas Archipelago

population

Only 6 islands are inhabited. The total population 5,419 inhabitants increases by 5% per year. All th villages are in the valleys. Taiohae, the capital, is o Nukuhiva, with schools, hospital, bishopric and por

access

By plane: There are two airports, one on Ua-Huka, on on Hiva-Oa. Air Polynesia flies there twice a week from Papeete. The flight takes 5 hours with a 15 min. stop a Rangiroa.
By boat: 2 ferries call regularly: the *Taporo III* leaves o no fixed date from Papeete. The trip takes 4 days.
The *Aranui* makes a 20 to 25 day return trip whic includes various stops in the Tuamotu.
With no fixed schedule, there are ferries that link th several islands, but the service is not guaranteed.

accommodation

Atuona village (Hiva-Oa). Guy Rauzy offers accommo dation with bar and restaurant.
Puamau (Hiva-Oa). Bernard Heitaa and Vohi Tanoa ca both offer 2 rooms.
Hane village (Ua-Huka). Vii Fournier has accommo dation.
Vai Paee village (Ua-Huka). Mme Miriama Fournier Mme Joseph Lichtle and Mme Laura Raioha hav houses to rent.
Taiohae village (Nuku-Hiva). Becfin restaurant has bungalows. Chez Mate et Fetu, Keikahanui Inn.
Vaitahu village (Tahuata). Naani Barsinas can offer three-roomed house. Boat trips possible and horse to rent.
Omoa village (Fatu Hiva). Joseph tetunuani, Franco Peter, Kehu Kania and Tehau Gilmore have each go houses to rent.

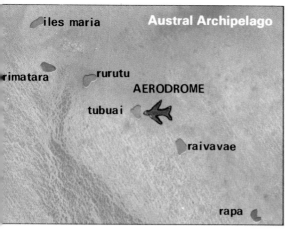

iles maria

rimatara

rurutu

AERODROME

tubuai

raivavae

rapa

access

By plane: There are airports at Tubuai and Rurutu. Air Polynésie has two flights a week: Tuesdays and Saturdays to both islands and Thursdays to Tubuai only.
By boat: The *Tuhaapae II* leaves Papeete once or twice a month for the Austral Islands (Rimatara, Rurutu, Tubuai, Raivavae), Ferries only call 3 or 4 times a year to Rapa.

tubuai

tubuai

Tubuai is a circular island, surrounded by a barrier reef. There is only one pass that can be used, in the north-east near Mataura village. The population is 1,410. The principal villages are: Mataura in the north, Huahine in the interior, Mahu in the south and Taahuaia in the north-east.

accommodation

Mme Caroline Tetuaearo has 5 comfortable bungalows to rent in Mataura.
M. Aumera has 4 bungalows 1 km from Mataura.
M. et Mme Tenepau rent two small houses.
The Ermitage Sainte Hélène belonging to Noel Ilari has 3 comfortable bungalows, near Mahu village.

useful information

Car hire and boats for deep sea fishing — contact the Mayor of Mataura
Bicycles, mobylettes and horses for hire — M. Ato.
Trips on the lagoon — M. Paipi.

cursions

ere are no organized excursions in the Marquesas, it it is always possible to hire a horse, as there are a w mountain paths.
• visit: Gauguin's tomb (he died in 1903) in Atuona metery, on Hiva Oa. See also Jacques Brel's tomb.
Archeological remains on Fatu Hiva, specially a *epae* in Omoa.
Virgin Bay, Hanavave, Fatu Hiva.
Traitor's Bay, Atuona and Hanaiapa Bay, Hiva Oa.
Archeological remains on Hiva Oa: *meae* and *epae,* platforms on which the *tiki* stood. The Teii-na *meae* were famous because of the height of eir *tiki.* The highest one is at Takaiki: 3.50 m.
Taiohae Bay must be seen at Nuku Hiva.

stral archipelago

e Austral archipelago lies 600 km south of Tahiti. includes 5 high islands (Tubuai, Rimatara, Rurutu, ivavae and Rapa) and 2 atolls (Hull and Bass). ey are of volcanic origin and not very high (100 to 0 m), except Rapa (highest point: 1,460 m). Rapa also the island farthest south.

pulation

e total population is 5,208. Five of the islands are abited. Rapa has the largest concentration of abitants, but Mataura, on Tubuai, is the capital, th the administrative centers, schools and hospital.

rurutu

accommodation

At the house of the mayor of Rurutu.
Catherine Ariiotima has rooms to rent in Moerai district, Rurutu, and rents out a jeep for trips around the island.
Hotel Rurutu Village, Avera.
Mme Atai Aape has a four rooms for rent, Moevai.

Climatically, the Austral archipelago is colder than the rest of French Polynesia, especially during the cold season, from May to October.

Printed in Japan
July 1983
Publisher's number: 194

The information section was prepared by Hélène Herrmann-Auclàir. The lay-out is by Jean-Louis Saquet, the maps are by Thierry Steff (End paper pages) and by Gilles Cauneau (Information section)

The photographers of **Tahiti and its islands** are:
Bernard Hermann: pages 4-5, 14-15, 17, 23, 28-29, 32-33, 36, 40-41, 46-47, 48, 50-51, 52-53, 54, 57, 58-59, 62-63, 64, 66-67, 68-69, 76-77, 80-81, 90-91, 96-97, 98 and 102-103.
Erwin Christian: Cover photograph and endpapers and pages 6-7, 8-9, 11, 16, 27, 34, 39, 55, 64-65, 81, 82-83, 84-85, 87, 88, 91.
Michel Folco : pages 20-21, 22, 24, 37, 38, 42-43, 49, 56, 75, 77, 78-79, 92-93, 99, 100-101, 105, 106-107 and 117.
Claude Rives: pages 12-13, 18-19, 34-35, 70-71, 74, 90, 108-109 and 110-111.
Others are by Jean Coquin (pages 50 top left, 82 bottom, 96 top and 97 top), Jean Tapu (page 10), M. Maitrot of Air Tahiti (page 26), Raymond Bagnis (page 104), and Pacifilm (pages 116 and 117 right).